PUPPY WISE

Creating a Harmonious and Lasting Relationship with Your Puppy

PUPPY WISE

Creating a Harmonious and Lasting Relationship
with Your Puppy

Danielle Gutelius
Owner of Tanager Akitas

Henschel
H A U S
publishing, inc.
Milwaukee, Wisconsin

The author is available for speaking engagements
and puppy owner coaching.
Contact Danielle@tanagerakitas.com

Published by:
HenschelHAUS Publishing, Inc.
2625 S. Greeley Street, Suite 201
Milwaukee, WI 53207
www.henschelHAUSbooks.com

ISBN: 978-1-59598-227-8
E-ISBN: 978-1-59598-304-6
LCCN: 2013935732

Photographs by the author and courtesy of Donald Nelson,
Inner Vortex Publishing.

Printed in the United States of America.

A portion of the proceeds from the sale of this book goes to Akita rescue.

*This book is dedicated to the memory of Breeze,
who deserved more from the people who loved her.*

*May this book serve to enlighten and inform
so that the misunderstandings of her needs
become understood and illustrate
how to create successful relationships
between dogs and the people who care about them.*

Table of Contents

Acknowledgments i

Introduction 1

Part 1: The Ideal Puppy
    1. What is the Ideal Puppy? 9
    2. Finding Your Ideal Puppy 13
    3. Preparing for the New Addition 23

Part 2: Understanding the Canine Perspective
    4. The First Couple of Weeks 27
    5. Fitting Into The Ranks 31

Part 3: Teaching Your Puppy
    6. Starting Off on the Right Paw 61

The Tail End 101

Additional Resources 103

About the Author 105

Acknowledgments

inding the courage to write my personal experiences and ideas in an official book has been a labor of love, overwhelming doubt, and a heaping dose of inner growth. It would never have happened without the many friends and associates who suggested and prompted me into doing it. Many thanks also to those who willingly read my early drafts, encouraged, and pushed me to complete it.

Thanks must be offered to my editor and publisher, Kira Henschel, for her endless patience and kindness while I journeyed along the path of bringing this book into the Light.

Most importantly, the biggest thanks goes to a bunch of characters who will never read these words, or even know that they have been acknowledged: the many dogs that have been part of and blessed my life over the last twenty years and provided the experiences, learning material, and many examples that are included in this book. Special recognition to Kissho, Ice, Willow, Glacier, Valor, and Breeze.

Introduction

Humans and dogs have been companions for thousands of years. While much has changed over our history together, the internal workings of the relationship have remained basically unchanged since we shared that first warm fire together. The bond between human and dog transcends mere physical companionship. More than any other animal, the dog has connected with us on an emotional level. One role many companion dogs now perform is to help us connect with our true selves. Through the love we feel for our canine companions, we are reminded of the good in the world and the good that lies in the heart of every person.

There are plenty of books that offer instruction on how to train your dog to be obedient and respond to commands. The intention behind this book is to provide insights that will give you a greater understanding of your dog—how it learns and how it relates to its world.

Dogs, as living, breathing beings, have their own feelings and emotions, as well as natural drives and unique personalities. From the first day you bring a puppy into your life, you are responsible for teaching it the necessary skills for living in your home and in the world. By learning to effectively communicate with your pet, you will establish the foundation for all its future learning.

Reputable, caring breeders put a lot of time and effort into the first several weeks of a puppy's life in order to lay the groundwork for it to become an outstanding family member. Based on my own observations and more than 20 years of hands-on learning with my own dogs, this guide was written to help you cultivate that relationship and raise your puppy with understanding, love, and common "dog sense." In doing so, you will enjoy the most fulfilling relationship you can experience with a canine companion—and probably one of the easiest relationships to create.

Perhaps as more people come to appreciate and understand what our dogs need from us and learn how to communicate with them, much of the confusion, disappointment, and heartbreak that all too often accompany dog ownership in our society will be eliminated. This heartbreak comes in the form of millions of animals being discarded and euthanized every year. National statistics estimate that 6 million to 8 million companion animals are adopted annually from shelters, with another 3 million to 4 million euthanized for lack of adoptive homes.

In this day and age, most people get a dog for companionship and the opportunity to care for a living creature with which to share an emotional bond and to experience unconditional love. Many people will say that their dogs are like their children. In just the past few decades, the role of most dogs has changed dramatically: from working-class animal with demanding jobs to perform to that of family member, friend, and constant companion.

When you make the decision to become a dog owner, it is important to remember that our dogs remain dogs: their DNA has not changed nor made them into some new creation. They have not become fur-cloaked, cold-nosed humans. By understanding our dogs as dogs, we can enjoy the close emotional and spiritual connection we wish to have with them.

By accepting and acknowledging a dog for its potential as a loyal, responsive, and loving companion, we can open the doorway to greater understanding and deeper respect for our canine friends. When our hearts open to our beloved dogs, our hearts will also open to the world and all the creatures in it.

Breeze's Story

Breeze was an Akita puppy from my very first litter. When Breeze went to her new home, she was 18 months old, and a sweet, submissive, willing-to-please young dog.

All went well at the beginning. After a couple of years, however, her owner reported she was occasionally growling and refusing to obey commands she knew well. Further information revealed Breeze was being overly indulged and allowed to do as she pleased, without correction or any effort to modify her attitude.

The owners were strongly advised to get Breeze under control and prevent her domineering displays from escalating. The warnings and suggestions on how to accomplish this went unheeded. Breeze's bad behavior continued for some more time. Finally, the phone call came that Breeze had bitten a family member, just when the owners had decided to engage a professional trainer to work with her. Unfortunately, they had waited too long.

After years of warning her owners through her actions and clearly telling her family that she needed firmer guidance and strict leadership, Breeze had crossed the line and assumed the role of Alpha.

The family was now completely unable to manage her. The trainer already had a similarly natured dog and couldn't take on another. The breeder (me) couldn't take her back due to the legal liability of keeping a known biter. Breeze was euthanized in the prime of her life.

What had been a docile, easy-going young dog turned into a dangerous, untrustworthy adult. Why? Because she had been spoiled, allowed to dictate her behavior, and became the ruling member of the household. Had her owners understood and provided the authority and guidance Breeze needed to remain the gentle soul she truly was, she could have grown old and lived in comfort for many more years.

Breeze's story is a sad example of how irresponsible and uneducated ownership results in heartbreak for owners and instances in which the dog pays the price with its life.

Spoiling a puppy does it no favors and is truly a disservice. All young animals require proper upbringing with boundaries and certain expectations. Owners need to understand how to take a leadership role with their puppy and maintain a proper hierarchal relationship throughout the dog's life. Doing so creates a rewarding and enjoyable relationship.

Breeze was the inspiration for the theme and content of this book. She will remain forever in my heart and memory.

Part 1:
The Ideal Puppy

1. What is the Ideal Puppy?

hat is the ideal puppy? It is a beloved companion that will fit comfortably into your family and be a joy to share your life with for the next ten to twenty years.

Your ideal puppy is just that—*your* ideal puppy—a puppy that fits into your life. You get to choose the lessons and requirements to teach your puppy that are important to you for creating a happy life together. If you want to have your puppy join you at the dinner table, then go for it. If you enjoy having your puppy sitting next to you on your sofa, then let it. You choose if you want your puppy to be an obedience pro or just understand the basics for living comfortably in your house.

Use the information in this book to understand how your puppy learns and why it does what it does. Armed with that knowledge, you will understand how to teach your puppy the concepts it needs to learn to become your ideal dog. These concepts are written as a broad, basic overview, with the understanding that every breed has its own general characteristics and every puppy has its own personality. Your puppy is an individual. Adapt and modify the techniques in this book as needed for your special puppy. A technique that works perfectly for a large-breed puppy may have to be adjusted for one of a smaller breed.

Respect and appreciate your puppy as it is and be realistic in your expectations. At just 8 weeks old, the typical age a puppy goes to its new home, your puppy is

joining your family and being taught a multitude of rules and regulations: what to chew, where to relieve itself, what and where is off limits, in addition to a bevy of new words. Add the stress of being plucked from the family it has known since birth and having to acclimate to a new family, and that's a serious and traumatic life change! Your puppy needs your patience and understanding and a minimum of six months to grasp the basic concepts. Many exasperating behaviors are part of your puppy's genetic makeup, which it simply needs time to outgrow.

Your puppy does not come pre-programmed for perfect behavior. Once you bring it into your home, you have accepted the responsibility of educating your puppy and being responsible for its well-being for the remainder of its life. It takes 20 years (usually longer) for a human to mature into a responsible, well-mannered adult who is enjoyable to be around—about one-fourth the typical lifespan. With a dog's average lifespan of 14 years, that is just over three years for a puppy to mature into a well-mannered dog that is a joy to have in your life.

Realize that it takes time for a puppy to truly grasp all the concepts and etiquette you want it to learn and display. Education, wisdom, and maturity do not happen overnight, or even in a few months. Your puppy needs years of nurturing and guidance to become the ideal dog for you.

The stronger your ability to speak your puppy's language, the easier it will be for your puppy to absorb what you are teaching. Understand how your puppy perceives and responds to the world around it. Your willingness to see the world from your puppy's point of view is what helps to create a meaningful relationship with your puppy and to open a path of clearer communication. Through you, as teacher and lifelong companion, your puppy will learn how to live in a human world. Accept and respect your puppy for the beautiful creature it is, and enjoy it for the love and companionship it brings into your life.

2. Finding Your Ideal Puppy

Nearly every puppy has the potential to be ideal if given the care and understanding it needs and deserves. The maxim that "there are no bad dogs" is true so long as the dog has been raised under positive conditions. A puppy should have a stable temperament, gained through the responsible breeding of two healthy animals. It also should be free of major health issues that could cause unnaturally aggressive or unstable behavior.

As it is nearly impossible to know if a puppy has or will develop serious health or temperament issues just from looking at it, buying from a reputable breeder whose deepest intention is to produce healthy puppies is the safest way to assure you will get a healthy puppy.

The way to begin looking for your ideal puppy is to first determine the breed that fits your lifestyle. There are over 165 breeds recognized by the American Kennel

Club. Each has its own "Breed Standard," which describes physical appearance and general personality traits, as well as the original function each breed was designed to serve.

Knowing a particular breed's function and purpose is fundamental to understanding its characteristics and thus whether or not a certain dog would be a good fit for you. An Irish Setter, for example, was bred to hunt birds and therefore has an enormous amount of energy and endurance for running far and wide in a field hunting its quarry. This dog is a far cry from a Pekingese, which was bred to be a companion, spending the bulk of its life sitting on its owner's lap.

Before bringing a puppy into your life, there is much to consider. First, you must take an honest look at your life and be certain you have the desire and ability to commit the necessary time to a puppy that will quickly grow into an adult dog. Second, make an informed decision about what breed of dog to acquire. Writing a list of the reasons for getting a dog and another list detailing the desired qualities is a good start.

Examples of questions to ask yourself and your family, or others who might be impacted by introducing a dog into the family:

- Are you willing to regularly groom a long-haired breed, or do you want the ease of a short-haired breed that requires little grooming?

- Do you want a dog for protection, companionship, a jogging partner, or all of the above?

- How much time do you have to offer an active dog the exercise it needs?

- Is your home big enough to accommodate a large breed, or do you need to get a small dog?

- Will it be just you and your dog, or will you need a highly social breed to fit into a home with children and constant visitors?

- Are you a person who loves the outdoors? If your dog is joining you on your outdoor adventures, is it built to endure various weather extremes?

- A humorous, yet important, question to consider: What sized poop pile are you willing to pick up several times per day?

There are plenty of other aspects to consider. By searching out and speaking with knowledgeable breeders who can advise you on the pros and cons of their breeds, you can gain a better understanding of a breed's characteristics, which in turn will help you to determine if your choice is the right breed for you.

You also must consider your skill level and familiarity with dogs. Honestly assess your ability to safely handle a breed with a dominant or challenging disposition. First-time dog owners are smart to avoid larger, dominant breeds; save this type of dog for when you have acquired the experience and a solid understanding of "dog sense." There are many avenues available to learn about breeds. Go to your local library for a dog encyclopedia that briefly describes each breed, surf the Internet, or attend a local dog show and talk to people. Find the breed or breeds that best suit you, and make a logical, informed choice.

Once you have done your homework and made the appropriate decision about which breed you wish to add to your life, you must decide where to obtain your ideal puppy. If you want to know where your puppy has come from, and be ensured that it was brought into this world with intention, conscientiousness, and love, you will want to find a reputable and responsible breeder from whom to purchase your ideal puppy.

Buying from a Breeder

Reputable breeders have a passion for their dogs. They care about the physical, mental, and emotional health of their animals. They have dogs because they enjoy the pleasure that their dogs offer them, whether it is through competition in the show ring, field trials, or various other sporting events.

These professionals adhere to a detailed written standard of the American Kennel Club (AKC) that describes in detail the physical appearance, general disposition, and purpose of all AKC-registered breeds of dog. A reputable breeder's first and foremost intention is improving the quality of their dogs through caring and responsible breeding practices. They are concerned not just with the appearance, but with the physical and emotional health of their animals.

Reputable breeders put extensive time and care into raising puppies, inside their homes, so that these little ones can grow into happy, well-adjusted dogs. They carefully screen, match, and place their puppies with the appropriate, devoted families. A responsible breeder will screen potential buyers as thoroughly as a buyer is screening the breeder. A few qualities a breeder may be interested in include:

- How well the potential buyer understands the breed of dog he or she is considering purchasing.
- Has the buyer done his or her homework?
- Does the buyer understand and accept the unique qualities of the breed?
- Has he or she owned the same breed of dog before?
- What is it about the breed that the buyer finds appealing?
- A breeder must know that the buyer has the correct home environment, the time, and the commitment to provide for the puppy for the duration of its life.

Using your local Yellow Pages or doing an Internet search, you are likely to find various kennel clubs. These organizations originally formed and continue to exist for the advancement and interest of purebred dogs. The committed and knowledgeable dog enthusiasts within the Club will often offer referrals on responsible breeders. They can also inform you of upcoming AKC–sanctioned dog shows in your area, which is a fun way to see many breeds all in one day and meet many knowledgeable dog professionals.

The Internet is also a good resource when searching for individual breeders who have chosen the World Wide Web as their advertising vehicle. However, because Web sites are also used as marketing and advertising tools, everything you read on an individual's site cannot be taken at face value.

It is crucial to take the time to meet the breeder from whom you are interested in purchasing a puppy. Visit with his or her dogs to gauge the temperaments of the animals. Also look for cleanliness and other indications that ensure the dogs are being cared for properly.

For personal safety and the safety of their dogs, many breeders prefer to meet puppy buyers somewhere other than their home, such as at a dog show. Some criteria to consider, based on where you are meeting the breeder and his or her dogs, are:

- All the dogs are in good health with no obvious signs of disease or injury.

- All the dogs are clean, well groomed and nails are trimmed short.

- The dogs' eyes are clear and bright and express inquisitive interest in visitors.

- The dogs joyfully interact with their breeder or owner.

- The area for the dogs is clean, with no overpoweringly offensive odors.

- The breeder is committed to quality, rather than quantity and profits.

- The breeder is excited to talk about the dogs' accomplishments and successes.

- The breeder willingly presents certificates of health tests on the dogs.

- All dogs have access to clean water.

- The dogs have an area available for play and exercise.

Very importantly, good breeders will exhibit pure love, affection, and concern for their dogs. You will know intuitively which breeders are committed to providing the very best for their dogs.

Pet Store Puppies

Buying a puppy from a pet store is a risky move. Puppies, as well as kittens, do not belong in stores. As highly social animals, they require affection and meaningful interaction to set the foundation for becoming well-adjusted companions—needs that cannot be met while sitting in a small cage, usually alone, with no person or other animal with which to develop a meaningful bond. Without experiencing such a connection, creating a bond in the future will require greater time and effort. A pet store offers no opportunity to meet a puppy's parents, to learn what conditions it was born into, or what health issues to be aware of.

The typical pet store employee has no knowledge of the various breeds and cannot advise you on what to expect from the puppy you buy, nor will you have any support or assistance after purchase. The bottom line is that pet stores are selling puppies for profit—not to serve the best interest of the puppy or the buyer. Knowledge, concern, and long-term dedication are what you want and will get from a reputable, responsible and caring breeder.

Adoption and Rescue Organizations

Many reputable breeders are also associated with their breeds' rescue organizations. These non-profit groups take in, shelter, foster, and "re-home" dogs that have been given up by their previous owners for various reasons. The rescue organizations screen potential adopters and match each dog with the person or family best suited for each particular dog in their care.

There are also many loving animals—purebreds and mutts—available for adoption at local animal shelters and capable of becoming your ideal dog. Adopting a puppy or dog from a shelter or rescue situation is different than getting a puppy from a breeder, as these canines generally come with a little or a lot of emotional baggage. Working through and around that baggage requires a different approach and will not be discussed here.

Puppies raised by breeders in a positive setting, provided with every opportunity to flourish, are virtually unblemished slates ready to be molded into ideal dogs by their new family. So, whether you opt to obtain a puppy from a breeder or a dog from a shelter or rescue situation, you will need to invest time and effort in building a relationship and teaching your canine companion proper etiquette.

Adding a dog or puppy to your life is an enormous responsibility and requires you to make a commitment that lasts for the lifespan of the dog—from 10 to 20 years depending on the breed you choose. Finding your ideal canine companion will be well worthwhile when you experience the joy that comes from a relationship with your ideal dog.

3. Preparing for the New Addition

Now that you understand the responsibility of adding a new, four-legged bundle of energy to your life, have determined what breed of dog best suits you, researched and located the source for attaining your puppy, and are committed to caring for it for the next decade or more, it is time to begin planning for its arrival.

Before your puppy arrives, it is important for you and every family member to agree on what behaviors will be allowed or not and what command words to use, so that everyone will be teaching your puppy the same rules and using the same cue words. Being consistent will help your puppy to learn its lessons and the meaning of words more quickly. Your puppy needs to receive the same message from everyone who will take part in teaching it, and learn to abide by one rule in any given situation.

Prior to bringing your puppy home, you will want to have the following items ready and waiting:

- A properly sized crate
- Food and water bowls
- Food, treats, and breeder-recommended vitamins
- Suitable toys
- Collar and leash
- Some old towels and an odor-eliminating cleaning product to clean up any mishaps
- Quick access to the name, address, and phone number of your veterinarian of choice

The next section of this book will help you understand canine behaviors and provide a basis from which to learn your puppy's language.

Part 2: Understanding the Canine Perspective

4. The First Couple of Weeks

For its first two weeks of life, a puppy is focused entirely on physical and mental growth. Newborn puppies respond to basic survival stimuli, such as temperature changes, feelings of hunger, and the presence of their mother, littermates, and human caretakers. At this stage, puppies cannot be trained; no amount of conditioning or reinforcement will create a learned response.

When a puppy is two or three weeks old, a fascinating change occurs as a puppy becomes aware of its surroundings and itself. It is heartwarming to watch a litter of puppies at this phase of life. Often, the first time a puppy barks, it will startle itself and fall down, or decide to repeatedly use its wonderful, new-found voice at 2 o'clock in the morning!

Littermates start to play with each other, establishing a hierarchy as their individual personalities emerge. At this stage, a puppy actually learns behaviors and training can begin to make the transition from littermates to human-mates pleasant for both the puppy and its new family.

Most of a puppy's self-concept is formed during its first three months of life, similar to the earliest days of a human baby's life, observing and taking it all in, with the brain making rapid-fire connections and storing data like a computer for future access.

This means the training techniques used by a breeder have an enormous impact on the puppy's future. These techniques can affect the basis for its behavior, habits, and nature over the course of its life. Consequently, the time and attention a breeder gives to a litter during these early weeks is vital. Puppies need to receive lots of human contact—such as being picked up and handled with regular touching and stroking over all areas of the their bodies. At this stage, puppies should also be exposed to various household noises: TV, vacuum, pots dropping, doors slamming, and so on, to get them used to the noises they will hear in their new homes.

As the puppies become more mobile, a breeder can acclimate them to different floor and ground surfaces—letting them walk on carpet, stones, and grass. A breeder could also walk the puppy alongside the road to get it used to the rumble and movement of automobiles.

A breeder's teaching a puppy to manage stairs during its first eight weeks, while it is utterly fearless, is of great benefit to a new owner, who will have a much tougher time teaching stairs to a three-month old puppy that has never navigated stairs before. The more encounters a puppy has had to normal, everyday occurrences within a human environment, the easier it will be for the puppy to adapt to life in its new home with new caretakers.

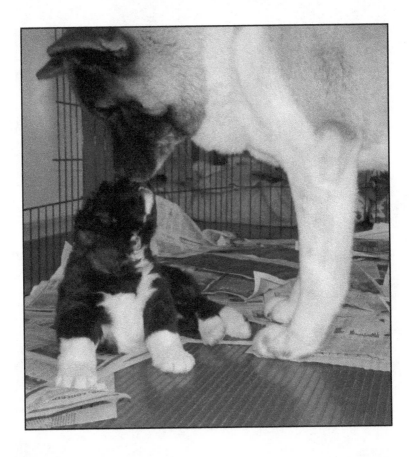

Example of body posturing during play

5. Fitting Into The Ranks

A puppy begins to determine its rank amongst its littermates from as early as three weeks of age, when it really begins to get on its feet and move around. A puppy will learn where it ranks by practicing dominant body posturing, rollovers and hold-downs, vocalization, and eye contact during wrestling matches.

When a puppy enters a new environment, like your home, it automatically begins to test the members of its new pack to find where it ranks. The actions and responses of family members will indicate to your puppy its position within the pack. Your goal is to have your puppy understand it has the least amount of authority within your family, which is accomplished easily through everyday interactions from the time your puppy arrives and continued through its life, and will be explained in the next few chapters.

Your puppy will continue to use various instinctive behaviors to assess its position for years to come, which is why it is so important for every human member of your family to understand your puppy's natural behaviors and to learn to react appropriately—from a position of authority. By doing so, your puppy will learn that it is the "Omega," the lowest-ranking member within the pack, which will reduce its inherent drive to rise to Alpha, or "top dog" status. If it's not clear who is in charge within your pack, your puppy may, over time, try to step into the Alpha role, thus making it important for you to establish the proper hierarchy right from the start.

Communicating with Your New Puppy

The next step in preparation for the addition of your ideal puppy is to delve into the canine psyche and learn how to effectively communicate with and educate your puppy. Be able to look at and understand situations from your puppy's perspective, and teach it by using its method of learning. This will make training enjoyable and incredibly easy. Expecting your puppy to learn via human-style communication practices, such as lengthy dialogue, sarcasm, and various non-verbal cues will prove impossible and frustrating for both you and your puppy, and will result in much more failure than success. Take the easy road: dog language is easy to understand and makes learning together fun!

As with any relationship, quality communication on every level is the prerequisite for success. Once clear communication with your puppy is achieved on the mental and physical levels, the emotional and spiritual connection will develop and deepen.

The basis of *quality communication* is accepting that your dog is more than just a physical body. Every animal possesses a life force, or soul, with emotions, intelligence, and individual personality. Connecting to your puppy on an emotional and spiritual level can be the vehicle through which you may know and experience true joy and complete acceptance from another living being.

Meaningful communication involves understanding how your dog operates in its world to allow you to understand its behavior from its perspective.

Respectful communication is teaching your dog in its language so that it will understand what you want it to learn.

When your puppy is brought home and starts to become a part of your family, even if the "family" is just you and your new puppy, it won't look at you as human or understand you as another person would understand you. Rather, your puppy responds and relates to you as if you were a dog. It will observe and interpret your body language and vocal intonations. It will assess behaviors during playtime and interactions among all of the family members, thereby figuring out the authority levels between you, all the family members, and itself.

All these elements are important to the mental and emotional maturation of your puppy—and they all mean very different things to your puppy than they do to you as a human being. When you fail to understand these things from your puppy's perspective, communication breaks down. It is this lack of understanding that lies at the root of most of the behavior problems that occur with companion animals. Understanding your puppy's language will increase its ability to understand you.

Fitting Into the Ranks

As the newest member of the pack, your puppy will automatically assume the position of lowest rank because it has entered new terrain with new pack members. Your puppy will look for guidance from the higher-ranking (human) members. Being the lowest-ranking member does not imply any negative or demeaning aspects, such as inferiority or unworthiness. A simple analogy is to think of the military: the lower ranks follow the instruction of the higher ranks. Ranking within the canine world is all about authority—who has it and who has to follow it!

Alpha Dogs

A puppy that is allowed to grow into a position of authority within its human family will control the subordinates as it sees fit. Being the Alpha of a human family is extremely stressful for a dog and, of course, very dangerous for its family. The Alpha dog will take charge and determine how things should go, make decisions made from its canine perspective and which apply to canines—not to humans. Obviously this results in chaos.

As an example, canine protocol requires the Alpha dog to be at the forefront when intruders come near the pack, or to investigate new situations, and then choose a response or course of action. Here is the human version: the UPS delivery person is at the front door to deliver a package.

If a family member that the dog perceives as being of lower rank walks in front of the dog to answer the door, the dog, acting as the superior member, may growl at or even bite the person who walked past it as a way of administering punishment for stepping out of line, beyond the Alpha's authority. Any stress stemming from being in charge will most likely be released through aggressive behavior, such as growling, snarling, snapping, and eventually biting.

An Alpha dog controls its pack members through intimidation. Typically, a dog that is in the process of rising in rank will begin ignoring commands and growling when it is pushed to obey. Over time, if these initial actions are not taken seriously or ignored, the dog's behavior will escalate in severity to where it may snap at or bite any family member who crosses its idea of what is acceptable.

What to do: Remove the stress—stand strongly in your Alpha position, and let your puppy remain in the Omega position, and you will have a happy, relaxed member of the pack. When your puppy understands its position, it will instinctively look to the superior members of the pack for rules and regulations, and willingly cooperate with clear guidance from its leaders.

Fitting Into the Ranks

Each human member of your family must earn his or her dominant position over your puppy. Just as in a pack of canines, it is every dog for itself. It is not the job of the pack leader to assign or enforce ranking when it comes to other family members. Your puppy will perceive the levels of rank amongst the group by constantly watching and assessing interactions and responses between all the members. You or another human in the family who is pack leader, and so on down the ladder of hierarchy, must attain his or her status in relation to your puppy. Your puppy must learn and accept the superior ranking of all the other human family members. Disciplining your puppy into respecting other family members is ineffective. It may work while you are there, but what happens when you are not? Respect must be earned—individually.

Proper puppy parenting of your puppy never needs to be a test of wills or incorporate harsh actions. You will find that using a gentle approach, mingled with calm determination and clear communication, will result in the quickest learning. Maintaining authority is achieved through reinforcement on a daily basis of simple and subtle actions, like asking for a gentle rollover during playtime, requiring the fulfillment of a command before receiving a treat (as simple as "sitting" when told), walking through a door first with your puppy following, and obeying other commands your puppy has successfully learned.

Rebellious outbursts or challenges to your authority, similar to human teenagers testing their boundaries, occur during a dog's adolescent or teenage period, between one and two years of age—the age when most dogs are handed over to shelters by their owners. A puppy of more dominant and intelligent breeds will remember every weakness you exhibited during its puppyhood. And the more weaknesses your puppy perceives, the more likelihood there is for it to attempt to assume or usurp the position of Alpha or "top dog" when it reaches adolescence. Therefore, the better you lay the ground rules and establish the correct hierarchy, the less likely confrontation will occur later.

Maintain patience during your puppy's adolescence. Know that it will grow out of this trying stage and settle into being a relaxed member of your family. Arrange your family hierarchy with you at the top position of the social order and your puppy at the lowest, the only proper and safe ranking for a dog living with a human family. Doing so will create the proper relationship structure necessary for a long, healthy, and happy life together.

Understanding Canine Dominance

Dogs live in a dictatorship, not a democracy. In the canine world, the pack leader would never make requests of nor seek approval from its subordinates. Dogs are not to be given a choice in their behavior in important issues. A dog that is given too much leniency in decision-making will eventually sense that the pack leader is too weak to lead or make decisions.

The dog will see this as an opening to become pack leader itself. Unchecked, it will start giving directions using subtle maneuvers to force its authority. Over time, its actions will become more bold and threatening, possibly even leading to the ultimate challenge: a physical confrontation.

Being the dominant dog or pack leader means that an individual canine has established itself as having the right to set the rules that govern the pack, the right to discipline those who do not obey the rules, and the right to reward those who do. The dominant animal also has the responsibility to care for and protect other pack members. The subordinates in the canine family unit instinctively follow the established rules and are eager to do what is required of them for the sake of the pack.

Keep in mind that canine pack behavior is not a relationship based on fear, but rather on respect and devotion to the survival and well-being of the whole. The dominant position is generally not won in battle, but through a series of body and vocal displays. Physical aggression is generally the last resort when a long process of body posturing and vocal communication has not established a leader.

Knowing and anticipating the needs of the pack is a fundamental role of the pack leader. By anticipating your puppy's needs and looking out for its best interests, you gain its respect and it will be more willing to leave you in the leadership role rather than try to usurp your position.

Observe your puppy's body language, and you will be able to "hear" what is being said to you. For example, when you are playing fetch and your puppy begins retrieving its toy more slowly, you are being told, "I'm tired." At that point, stop the game and allow time for rest.

Or, your puppy hesitates during play and looks at its water bowl, direct your puppy to get a drink. Similarly, if you see your puppy is stressed or overwhelmed with the attention and petting from several people at one time, remove it from the situation or ask the people to stop. This shows your puppy that you are caring for it as its leader; you are in charge and addressing its needs. Your puppy will trust and honor your authority for looking after its well-being.

Being the dominant dog does not necessarily mean an animal is the biggest, smartest, or strongest, any more than being the subordinate one is the smallest, dumbest, or weakest. If this were the case, by virtue of our size and intellectual abilities, we humans could never be dominated by a five-pound Chihuahua. But that is oftentimes the case.

General ignorance of canine behavior results in people being intimidated more frequently by small dogs than larger ones. Small dogs often dominate and rule in their human households because they are seen as no threat even if they were to act aggressively, and are easily picked up and subdued by force. Dealing with a tiny terror may be easy for an adult, but children will have more difficulty handling authoritative little dogs.

Dogs do not assess their opponents the way we humans do: The average-sized person is quite likely to back down from a fight with a muscle-bound weightlifter type. But a pint-sized Min Pin will have no qualms about challenging a Doberman! With dogs, it is all about attitude. Logic would dictate that a Doberman would make quick work of a little Min Pin that dared challenge it. But the fact is that the posture, determination, and dominant attitude of the Min Pin can convey such a powerful message that the Doberman will back down and take the subordinate position! In such a scenario, the Doberman is responding canine to canine—and size doesn't matter in the world of dogs.

By understanding how your puppy instinctively operates within the hierarchy of its canine social structure, you open a clearer line of communication. Dogs respect and respond to a strong, confident leader—be one for your puppy and it will easily recognize, understand, and respond to your guidance and leadership when you communicate speaking its language.

Communicating Through Body Language

Canines communicate primarily by using body language. A dog can perceive the slightest tension or most subtle change in facial expression you display. For example, let's say you discover that your favorite cushion has been ripped to shreds earlier by your new four-legged companion. Your puppy senses your anger and begins acting submissively by lowering its tail, hunching down into a ball, and making itself look smaller. This is an inherent response in all puppies, and continues as an adult, as a natural reaction which generally works to diffuse the leader's hostility and bring harmony back to the pack.

Your puppy will not make the connection that its previous action—shredding the cushion—caused you to be angry. So it behaves submissively because it perceives your anger—not knowing the cause—and is seeking the return of your relaxed, approving attitude. In such a situation, there is little to be done. Reprimanding your puppy for shredding the cushion will only serve to confuse and frighten it. The immediate connection from its perspective, if you admonish it, is that punishment is the response for acting submissively—its last immediate action. You can imagine the confusion that would create!

Your response should be to take a deep breath and relax, console and reassure your puppy, and realize that it is not ready to be left alone or unsupervised. Perhaps, in a few more months, after further guidance and understanding of desired expectations, your puppy can be trusted to respect your personal possessions.

Your puppy is able to sense your emotions and general inner state, no matter what image you try to project. Because of this, it will know whether or not you are serious in giving a command. When your puppy has begun to learn commands, it may perfectly understand the command to "sit," but if you say it with your body half-turned, paying no real attention, and in a wishy-washy tone, your puppy will probably ignore you. On the other hand, if you are looking intently at your puppy, with your body held solidly, ready to take action, giving the command in a firm voice, with every intention of enforcing it, your puppy will see the determination in your body posture and obey.

Your Puppy's Learning Process

Canines learn "in the moment." You must observe and then stop undesired behaviors as your puppy is exhibiting them—and not a moment after. If you fail to catch your puppy in the act, take a deep breath and let it go, because correction even 10 seconds after the act is too late. Your puppy will not understand it at this point. Instead, simply commit to being diligent in observing your puppy and quicker to correct it the next time around.

Because your puppy learns by the immediate consequences of its actions, good or bad, you could unwittingly teach it a bad habit. Take this scenario: Your puppy is on your lap for a grooming session. It isn't particularly fond of this activity, so it twists and squirms out of your grasp and runs off: Success! (it thinks). Just like that, it learned how to avoid grooming and will consistently repeat this behavior. You are responsible for teaching your puppy to accept being groomed, so one way for you to succeed in this scenario would be to have a collar and lead on your puppy so it cannot get away. After a few sessions, it will learn there is no escape and accept the routine without a fuss.

By focusing on and determining the outcome of every action, you take an active role in your puppy's learning process. The times when you are not with your puppy and an event occurs, it will learn on its own via the positive or negative result of its actions. For example, if your puppy is sprayed by a skunk, presumably it will never tangle with a skunk again.

Your puppy learns just as quickly when it enjoys a positive outcome. Behavior resulting in a positive outcome will be repeated, such as knocking over a garbage can full of yummy leftovers to be enjoyed. Once a positive outcome has been experienced, it will be much more difficult to convince your puppy not to repeat its actions. Typical punishment in this type of situation has little effect because your puppy's focus is on the garbage can and its contents, which means that the negative consequence is coming from a different source (you) than what its attention is on (the garbage goodies).

Preventing undesired behaviors from occurring is much easier than trying to change your puppy's thinking after it has already enjoyed a rewarding, pleasurable experience. In this situation, teach your puppy that the garbage can is off-limits the moment it discovers the garbage.

Because you are watching your puppy every moment it is loose, when you see it express interest in the contents of the garbage can, immediately draw its attention to you, offering praise the moment its focus changes from the garbage to you. Be consistent in doing this each time your puppy becomes interested in the garbage, and very soon, it will learn that leaving the garbage alone results in your loving attention and, occasionally, a treat as well. It really can be that simple. Just think of the many different situations this easy technique can apply to. Even better is to avoid this situation altogether and simply put the garbage where your puppy is unable to get at it. The easiest solution is usually the best solution!

The garbage can scenario is a perfect example of how communication breaks down between human and dog. Humans all too often believe dogs are capable of logical thought or of rationalizing and connecting a bad behavior, such as knocking over the garbage while the owner is not watching, to the punishment received when the owner later finds trash all over the floor. The truth is a dog is incapable of connecting these two events. If such behavior becomes repetitive, your dog will learn that garbage on the floor leads to punishment—NOT that the act of dumping the garbage is what leads to punishment.

How often have you heard a dog owner say, "My dog does such and such out of spite whenever I leave the house," followed by, "He knows what he did because he acts guilty when I walk in the door"? "Spite" and "guilt" exist for humans, not canines. Rather, if a puppy was left unsupervised and dumping the garbage was allowed to become a habit, when it sees the garbage on the floor, it has learned that punishment results, and so it goes into a submissive posture as soon as the owner walks into the house.

During the first, most impressionable year of your puppy's life, you must pay attention to everything you are teaching it. Unlike your puppy, you have the capacity to instantly observe a situation, assess the possible outcomes, and determine the desired result and how to achieve that result. When teaching, keep your thoughts and reactions in the moment, as in the following example:

Your puppy inquisitively picks up a rock. Of course, you are concerned your puppy will choke or swallow the rock, causing gastric complications, requiring emergency surgery to remove the rock… Stop! Do you see how your thoughts have gone seriously beyond the moment? As you see your puppy pick up the rock, tell your puppy "out" and if necessary, pull the rock from its mouth. The instant the rock is out of your puppy's mouth, offer enthusiastic praise.

Avoid making the mistake of continuing the admonishment for picking up the rock due to your fears of "what could happen." Being in the moment, and offering praise the instant your puppy releases the rock, makes it more likely that your puppy will never pick up a rock again. The point is to stay focused in the present moment, just as your puppy does. You will begin to see life from its point of view of learning in each and every tiny moment. Offer praise, correction, or distraction appropriately. When you think like a dog, your puppy will respond to you more easily and learn more quickly.

Positive Reinforcement

Dogs are pack animals that want to live peacefully within the group structure, understanding the rules and how they fit in. That very nature makes them willing and eager to learn the rules of their pack, and it is the responsibility of the pack leader—you—to provide instruction.

Fitting Into the Ranks

Adult dogs use very gentle techniques to stop a puppy from doing something undesirable. Let's be honest: dogs are a lot less demanding and critical than humans. When an adult dog has had enough of a puppy's antics, it may immobilize the puppy by gently yet securely using its mouth to grab and hold the puppy still, sending a very clear message of who's in charge and that playtime is over.

Walking away from a playful puppy to a quiet spot is another way for an adult to stop play—and if the puppy persists—a little growl to make its point never hurts. A puppy investigating an adult's food or toys may be met with a gentle push from the adult, who uses its muzzle to forcibly push the puppy away.

Your puppy will follow all the rules once it understands them. If your puppy repeatedly does something you do not want it to do, it means you haven't yet instructed it in a manner it understands. It is not disobeying—it simply hasn't grasped the concept! It is your responsibility to find a different way to teach your puppy, and the most effective way is to reinforce acceptable behavior rather than punish bad behavior.

A puppy that has been raised with punishment and force is less stable and trustworthy because education using fear and punishment is a human method of teaching and demanding obedience. Dogs that have been raised using a punishment method are usually the dogs that are considered stubborn, difficult, or just plain "bad." Unruly dogs are typically the result of miscommunication, an inability of the owner and dog to understand each other.

Your puppy is a fun-loving creature. When something enjoyable follows any given situation, even an activity it isn't particularly fond of can be tolerated and ultimately enjoyed. With fun as a consequence—a treat, playtime, affection—whatever you teach your puppy will be repeated. Using positive reinforcement in accordance with your puppy's natural tendencies is using "dog language," to which your puppy is more responsive.

To make learning easier and faster for your puppy, search for ways to convert negative behaviors into positive ones. For example, your puppy is tempted by a tasty-looking chair leg and begins gnawing on it. Your calm and loving reaction is to gently push your puppy away from the chair leg and in the same moment, offer an acceptable chew toy for it to grab on to. As soon as your puppy bites onto the chew toy, lavish it with praise. In this case, you haven't changed the behavior of chewing but rather redirected it from a negative—a gnawed chair leg, to a positive—chewing on a suitable toy.

Distraction as Positive Reinforcement

Distraction is a form of positive reinforcement. While your puppy is in the midst of an undesired behavior, call it to you and offer praise the moment its focus changes. You have thereby positively reinforced the attention of your puppy to be on you.

You can reinforce every positive behavior your puppy is doing on a regular daily basis, such as offering quiet, gentle praise when your puppy is sitting quietly or lying down. By doing so, you are giving your puppy the message that being calm and quiet is desirable, which will encourage your puppy to repeatedly behave in that manner.

Consider this as well: Your puppy's antics are playful, silly, and wonderfully amusing. If you laugh and encourage your puppy, it is learning that whatever it is doing to attract your positive attention is acceptable. Realize that you are in the process of creating a fun, yet possibly mischievous, companion. You merely need to understand what you are teaching and realize that what your puppy learns in youth will be continued as an adult. You must accept the consequences of the education you give your puppy and don't blame it for behaviors exhibited at the age of ten months that you encouraged at the adorable age of ten weeks.

Keep an Eye on Your Puppy

While your puppy is learning the basics of life in a human house, it is imperative to observe it at all times while loose, or restrain it in a safe place, such as its crate, where there is no opportunity to learn bad behaviors. It must be emphasized that dogs do not understand human-style punishment—which fails to provide instruction to the dog of what is wanted.

Excessive yelling at or striking a dog only creates fear and has the potential to bring forth its aggressive, defensive instincts. With any breed—and especially the inherently dominant and tenacious breeds—tapping into their aggressive nature should be avoided at all cost. Every effort put forth to encourage your dog's sweet, friendly nature will be rewarded exponentially in creating a trustworthy, faithful, loving companion.

Everyone Agrees to the Rules

For your puppy to learn the rules of the pack, you and every other family member need to know and understand the rules you will live by with regard to raising your puppy. Doing so enables everyone to properly teach and enforce the rules uniformly and avoid confusing your puppy. It is unfair to your puppy if its willingness to comply is contradicted by being encouraged to jump on the couch by one family member, and admonished for doing so by a different family member.

Design your rules of etiquette and acceptable behavior based on what you want from your adult dog. Any rule that is expected of your adult dog must be taught and enforced while that soon-to-be adult is still a puppy.

The Importance of Socialization

We live in a highly social world. Puppies need to learn social skills and etiquette to fit in. You are the instrument through which your puppy will learn these necessary skills. The amount of dedication and commitment you put into the first year of raising your puppy will result in a tenfold return when you have a properly socialized and educated dog.

Early and frequent socialization is an important part of preparing your ideal puppy to be a relaxed and happy member of your family. After your puppy has developed a sense of security in its new home, probably 1 to 2 weeks after it arrives, begin visiting different locations that offer an array of sounds, noise levels, and distractions for it to experience and become accustomed to. Expose it to people of every size, shape, and color, and introduce it to all the people you expect to have entering your home.

When you introduce your puppy to new people, never scold it for exuberant behavior. Always encourage friendly acceptance of strangers. Allow your puppy to set the pace when meeting new people. Socializing means more than just having a multitude of people pet your puppy. The purpose of socializing is to have your puppy learn to be comfortable and confident when meeting strangers. You want your puppy to approach people willingly and choose to interact with them. To force your puppy to endure attention it doesn't seek can backfire as your puppy matures.

Dogs, just like people, have a sense of personal space. If a puppy's space is invaded repeatedly, it may start to defend that space. A puppy could start to back away from people and possibly begin growling. As its actions achieve the desired effect of keeping people at bay, the behaviors may become more extreme, such as barking, to ensure its success of safeguarding its space.

Successful socialization results from allowing your puppy to make the first move and approach people according to its comfort level. By praising and offering treats every time it chooses to seek attention from new people, you are conditioning a positive behavior in your puppy that is likely to continue into adulthood.

Should your puppy be so outgoing that it persistently jumps up, refrain from admonishing it for doing so, as it may connect strangers with the scolding and become unfriendly toward people. Always encourage and positively praise a puppy that is excited to greet people. You can prevent jumping by applying light pressure on its shoulders and chest and/or holding its collar. With patience and repetition, your puppy will soon learn to keep all four paws on the ground.

Be vigilant when introducing your puppy to people and keep all interactions safe and positive. During the first year, you must prevent potentially damaging encounters that could affect its personality later in life. Prevent small children from picking up your puppy to avoid it being dropped, which could lead to fear of children. A bad experience with an overly rough-handed man could create a fear of men. A puppy that has a traumatic experience with a particular type of person may apply that fear to every person who fits into that category.

You certainly want your puppy to be friendly toward people—even if your goal is to have it become a protection or guard dog. This advice may sound contradictory, but it makes abundant sense from a canine standpoint. Dogs are naturally inclined to protect their family and their home territory. Some breeds will even protect youngsters from parents and partners from each other. Your goal is to make the best use of this natural quality.

A dog reacts to that which is different—things it didn't become accustomed to while a puppy. As an example, a person wearing a hat is shaped differently than a person without a hat. That difference alone triggers a response in many dogs, especially poorly socialized ones. Through socialization, your puppy learns to accept people in all their variety, and will grant you peace of mind when you are in a social setting.

Your puppy is likely to be excited about every person it meets, but depending on the breed, it may become more reserved as it matures, and less receptive to overt affection. A characteristically dominant breed of dog will not be receptive to strangers hugging it, putting their faces in the dog's face, or holding direct eye contact. Most dogs interpret these postures as a challenge, causing it to become defensive. How would you feel about a stranger saying "Hello" and then grabbing you in a headlock? Not too kindly, surely. A dog will give warning by stiffening its body or growling, and if the unwelcome attention is not stopped, the dog could make efforts to defend itself. It is your responsibility to be observant and prevent any such situation from happening. Be proactive, know your dog, and avoid situations that you know it will take offense to.

Certain breeds were bred for the specific purpose of providing protection and guarding, which come with the qualities of independence and intelligence. If you choose one of these breeds, it is extra-important to make sure your puppy is well socialized—allowing your puppy's innate talent for assessing a dangerous situation to develop into a reliable asset that you can trust to keep you safe.

Know the difference between *protective* and *aggressive* behavior. A protective dog is a reliable, friendly, responsive guardian. An aggressive dog is one that expresses unwarranted violent behavior and is a walking liability, possibly even posing a threat to its own family.

To properly socialize your puppy, learn its characteristic breed traits, understand its unique personality, and accept the responsibility of protecting it, even from itself if need be. Respect it as a living creature with its own emotions, feelings, and inherent personality traits.

Do not subject your puppy to undesired attention and behavior from people you know it will be unreceptive to. No animal should have to tolerate abuse, teasing, or any such nonsense from anyone. As a responsible owner, you must accept this condition of dog ownership and ensure that as your puppy matures, it is kept out of situations where it may react in a defensive or threatening way. Respecting its individuality and personality is part of the joy of having a dog in your life.

At the Dog Park

Socializing your puppy at a dog park is ill-advised for many reasons. In a setting with many other dogs, you have very little chance of maintaining control of the situation. You will be unable to control the other dogs approaching your puppy and you certainly won't be able to control those dogs' owners or how they handle their dogs.

Your puppy could be subject to a dangerous and negative interaction with another dog. Your puppy could suffer the negative effects of such a confrontation for years to come. Or, if your puppy is of a dominant breed and is provoked by another dog, it could turn on the proverbial light switch of antagonism towards other dogs that can never be switched off, but will need to be managed for the remainder of your puppy's life.

When you consider that your overall goal in raising your puppy is to teach it how to live successfully in a human household, allowing it to romp uncontrollably with other dogs has the effect of teaching your puppy how to behave in a dog pack, which is quite different from how you want it to behave in your human pack.

As a dog owner, it is your responsibility to avoid and prevent, to the best of your ability, negative interactions and to protect your puppy from undesired or dangerous situations. It is in your and your puppy's best interests to be in settings where you can maintain control at all times. Dog parks do not offer a safe or controlled atmosphere. If you are determined to have your puppy play with another dog, make play dates with a friend's dog whom you trust and where both owners are able to agreeably control the play between the dogs.

Part 3: Teaching Your Puppy

6. Starting Off on the Right Paw

Grooming

During the first eight weeks of a puppy's life, cleanliness, nutrition, and lots of love and affection are the most important needs for a breeder to fulfill. Puppies that receive an abundance of positive human attention early on grow to become very people-oriented dogs that live comfortably with their human families.

An important physical routine that is begun by the breeder when the puppy is around one week of age is to begin trimming toenails. Frequent trimming serves to keep the puppy's feet set firmly on the ground for proper development and traction, and eliminates that annoying clicking sound when the puppy walks on hard flooring.

Continue the routine of weekly toenail trimming for the rest of your dog's life, for its physical comfort and as a training technique for proper behavior during regular grooming and care. Your puppy may wiggle, whine, or lightly mouth your hand the first few times you trim its toenails, but DO NOT give up on your mission. If it succeeds in thwarting you, this type of behavior could expand and lead to more undesirable behaviors. If necessary, have another person assist by holding your puppy, or make it even easier on yourself by doing it when your puppy is asleep or at least tired and less likely to put up a fuss. Remain patient and gentle; your puppy will soon learn to accept this routine.

Trimming Toenails

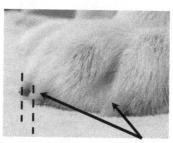

Quick   Cutting lines   Quick

1. Place the toenail clippers on the nail at a slight angle where the nail becomes thinner and curved, and clip. By removing the tip of the nail following a vertical line as shown, the nail is prevented from curving over and down, and will remain neat and short. A small

Dremel-type grinding tool can be used as well, which allows greater control, reducing the risk of cutting the *quick*, the blood vessel inside the nail. A Dremel tool can be purchased from most pet supply stores or your local hardware store.

2. With a black toenail, after trimming off the tip, the inside will be white. When you see a black dot in the center of the white, stop trimming—that's the quick!

3. With a white toenail, the inside will also be white, but the quick will be a pink dot. Often, white nails are clear enough to see through to the pink quick inside, making it easier to gauge how far to trim back the nail.

Maintain regular grooming and toenail-clipping sessions throughout your puppy's life. Inspect ears, teeth, and eyes. Teach your puppy to be comfortable with handling and examination, which comes in handy and is greatly appreciated during visits with the vet or the groomer.

Wiggly Dogs

If your puppy is being wildly unruly and no other option works, gently yet firmly cup its head while making direct eye contact. Hold this position until the puppy relaxes. You can also push your puppy into a down position by placing a hand on its shoulder and rump, if necessary, holding the puppy still until it calms down and stops squirming.

Mother dogs will often use their mouths on a puppy's head or neck to control and hold it in place, or pin it to the ground when the puppy's play gets too rough, or to control the puppy's biting. There is no harm to the puppy, because a mother dog uses her mouth very softly while sending a very clear message.

Give praise and release when your puppy settles. When holding an unruly puppy, make direct eye contact, looking intently into its eyes until it looks away, then praise. A puppy that is temporarily excited and hyper usually calms down if you turn your back and/or walk away. A puppy can have pent-up energy that needs to be released—just like a small child.

Let your puppy get the energy out of its system without recourse, perhaps by letting it run at will in your yard, and then you can both relax. If your puppy has too many episodes of crazed activity, you may need to provide more exercise on a daily basis during playtime to allow that energy to be released in a more positive manner.

The Motherly Roll

A helpful technique to begin with newborn puppies—and continue well into adulthood—is a gentle rollover. Its purpose is twofold: 1) It establishes trust between you and your puppy, and 2) sets up the proper authority structure in a non-threatening, loving manner.

While playing with your puppy, you can carefully roll it over on the floor or onto your lap, gently holding it in this position on its back, massaging, scratching, and running your hands over its entire body. Most puppies during playtime roll over regularly; it is at these times when you simply assist the puppy in rolling softly into a

Motherly roll

position on its side or back that it is already inclined to assume.

This position is comfortable for your puppy because from birth, its mother would roll it onto its back to lick and clean it—a pleasant experience. However, it is also a submissive position, placing your puppy in a state of vulnerability with its underbelly and throat exposed. For your puppy to feel relaxed and comfortable in this position, it must learn to trust you—even if held beyond its will. This technique allows you to mimic and take the place of your puppy's mother and will help to communicate that you are in charge, which helps prevent any major battles over that subject in the future. This simple technique sets the foundation for a proper and enjoyable relationship, one based on mutual trust and respect rather than fear and punishment.

The massage portion accustoms your puppy to being handled. You want your puppy to accept being touched on every area of its body. The regular caress of every toe or lifting the skin on the muzzle to examine teeth, in addition to the customary scratch behind the ear, is very important. If you ignore these or other areas of the body, your puppy will become shy of touch on those areas, meaning you will be in for a struggle when you need to attend to them.

Going slowly and carefully over your puppy's body as you massage it provides a health benefit as well. You will become familiar with its normal temperature, as well as muscle and bone structure. You can then recognize abnormalities such as tender spots, inflammation, or cysts—prompting simple first aid treatment or a visit to the vet.

Having your puppy accept this rollover maneuver is an excellent indication that your puppy trusts you and is comfortable with you putting it into a vulnerable position. Continuing to roll your puppy into a position onto its side or back throughout its life, as a regular part of playtime or petting, is a good way to consistently reinforce your position as the top dog and fortify the bond of trust between you.

Dominant Behavior

The following suggestions are to help you impart valuable lessons to your puppy. The correct responses to your puppy's actions clearly convey its position as the Omega, the lowest on the so-called totem pole. Keep in mind that this section discusses human-dog interaction, and that certain breeds are more inclined to exhibit dominant behavior as they mature.

Dominance disputes between dogs are beyond the ability of the average dog owner to control. Dogs that are inherently dominant toward other animals must be handled with great care. Human intervention is rarely successful in making dogs live peacefully together when the dogs are equal in temperament, each believing itself to be the next-highest ranking member below the pack leader, or any other family member. When dogs have an equally matched desire to be the top dog, a fight may ensue. These are no-win situations that can result in serious injury for one or both dogs and any person trying to separate them.

Understand also that this information relates to a *dominant* dog, rather than an *aggressive* dog, although both personality types may result in a dog that bites. An aggressive dog will bite for no apparent reason and should only be in the care of a professional, or it should be euthanized before serious injury occurs. A dog that behaves in a dominant manner toward people is oftentimes a sweet animal in wolf's clothing. It most likely has been spoiled by getting its way and has put itself in charge through intimidation. This situation can be changed with the proper education and commitment of its owners.

It's worth mentioning that physical correction might become necessary in the event of overly challenging behavior, such as baring teeth or snapping. Any such correction must be immediate and forceful enough to make an impact with the hope that it only takes one time for the dog to learn that such behavior will not be tolerated. If a situation has escalated to this point, it is best to call your breeder or a professional trainer for proper guidance.

Examples of dominant behaviors and how to counter them:

- Your puppy pushes its hip or shoulder into your body with obvious intention, as a maneuver to display its dominance. Counter by giving a little push back on its shoulder or hip. Do the same if your puppy purposely walks into you—gently step forward with your leg pushing into its chest and forcing it to take a step backward. By countering your puppy's actions, you convey that you are aware of the intention behind its action.

- Your puppy purposefully places its paw on you in a request for attention. You, as the one in the position of authority, grant attention at your behest. Because you want to give your puppy affection and love, you can gently push its paw off or place your hand on top of it before you begin to offer attention.

  Similarly, if your puppy stands up and puts its front paws on you or on the furniture, immediately and gently push on its chest, forcing it back onto all fours. As you push your puppy back, be consistent in gently voicing a command such as "off" at the same time. Once the puppy has all four paws on the floor, give praise immediately.

- Your puppy steps in front of you and is getting underfoot. To correct your puppy and keep you from tripping over it, put your hand on the puppy's chest and gently push it into a position behind or next to you. Be first in going through a doorway and make your puppy wait to go last. You can accomplish this

by placing your hand on the puppy's chest, thereby holding it in place, while at the same time giving a command, such as "wait." Once you step through the door, say "ok" and let
it follow.

- Your puppy attempts to take a toy or other object from you. If it's an object your puppy is allowed to have, make your puppy sit and then offer the item. Do not allow your puppy to take something without your OK. By handing your puppy acceptable chew toys, you teach both etiquette and indicate which items it is allowed to have. If your puppy grabs an item, retrieve it from your puppy, and then re-offer the item, praising when your puppy takes it nicely from you.

- Your puppy may try to push you out of a space you are occupying. Never get up to make room for it. Hold your ground. If you puppy attempts to sit or lie on you as a means of pushing you out, just push your puppy over a little and let it sit or lie next to you. On occasion, as a tool to enforce your leadership position, make your puppy get up from its spot on the floor, forcing it to give up its space to you. Then sit down where your puppy was.

- Refrain from chasing after your puppy in order to pet it—this is especially important for children. Let the puppy come to you for attention. If your puppy does not want attention, leave it alone. Chasing after a puppy is taking the submissive position from the puppy's point of view. The more space you give your puppy, the more it will come to you. In the canine world, the Omega regularly approaches the Alpha for reassurance.

- When playing a game of "chase," your puppy should be chasing you the majority of the time, not vice-versa. The dominant position in a game of chase is to be in front, directing the game. Always stop the game prior to your puppy losing interest or getting tired. In doing so, you remain in charge by making the decisions—and it will keep your puppy coming back for more the next time the game begins.

  Should your puppy ever get away from you, you are more likely to recapture it by walking away—your puppy will not want to be left behind and will be likely to run to you. You want your puppy to follow you, since you are the leader and it's unlikely you will ever be fast enough to chase after and catch your puppy if you needed to.

- A submissive dog will allow you to step over it and stand over it with your legs on either side for a brief period, without attempting to immediately get up or bound away. Any time you are in a position over your puppy with it relaxed and staying put, it is accepting your authority.

You do not need to be in the position of authority every moment of every day with your puppy. Occasionally, it is acceptable to allow your puppy to be in the Alpha (dominant) position while playing—such as during a game of chase or gentle wrestling. When your puppy is able to express its excitement and play full-on without reprisal, it will enhance the bond between you and build a greater level of trust. Your puppy will respect your authority when you incorporate little reminders throughout each day—as part of your regular communication which develops into a way of life.

Training Techniques

There is an array of gadgets, theories, and techniques available for use in training dogs. The common-sense approach is often forgotten amid all the hype of the "greatest new method." Patience and understanding remain the best tools to use for puppy rearing.

When you consider trying a suggested method, ask yourself whether you would use it to teach a human child. In many cases, the obvious answer is "no." Would you use a shock collar on a child to teach basic good behavior? Would you spray a child with an unpleasant solution to stop it from screaming or crying? Probably not.

One technique that works in a positive manner and is immensely effective is clicker training. Please see the Additional Resources at the end of this book to find more information on clicker training.

The proper use of treats is an important tool to achieve quick and lasting results. Tiny treats offered as a reward to reinforce a job well done makes training much more fun for your puppy and easier for you. Used correctly, treats are never the equivalent of a bribe. When offered in the moment of positive behavior, the treat encourages your puppy to repeat its actions.

Extreme training techniques may be appropriate in situations where a dog must quickly be taught a particular lesson for its own safety and well-being, or to correct a specific behavior that is detrimental to those around it. Professional trainers are available to assist in serious situations that require expert knowledge.

When you are interacting with your puppy, be mindful of the degree to which you are offering praise or correction. Begin with the mildest expression and notice how well your puppy responds. If there is virtually no response, at the next interaction raise it up a notch. Continue doing this until you find just the right level of excitement or admonishment to achieve the desired result.

Every puppy has its own internal programming for how much it will take to trigger a response. Use no more effort than is necessary as doing so may overly excite or unnecessarily frighten your puppy. Why yell when a whisper will do? Finding the precise level of communication is another piece of understanding canine language and developing good "dog sense." Incorporate with patience, tolerance, and love, and you have the ideal "technique" for raising your puppy.

Using Your Voice

Perhaps you have listened to two or more dogs at various times and in different circumstances. Dogs at play will bark at each other in a high-pitched tone and even include whining sounds. However, those same dogs that are protecting their property will voice a deep, low-pitched bark and some rumbling growls.

With that in mind, the way you use your voice is one of the most important training tools you possess. Be thoughtful of how your puppy reacts to the different pitch and tone of your voice. A high-pitched voice conveys excitement and play, but overuse it and you are on the road to creating a hyper dog. To you, that voice says how much you love your puppy, how wonderful it is, and how happy you are just being in its presence. If you talk to your puppy that way when you arrive home from work or whenever you are around it, your puppy could become overly excited and act uncontrollably. This leads to behaviors such as jumping up, excessive barking and whining, excessive salivation, and involuntary urination due to excitement.

Talk to your dog in a normal tone. Your eyes and soft facial expressions will tell it how much you love it. If you are calling your puppy to you, lift your voice to add enthusiasm and show praise for its response.

Be mindful of your tone of voice and how it affects your puppy. Use your voice in a manner that elicits the behavior you would like. For the most part, talk to your puppy in a normal, conversational tone. Use an excited, high-pitched voice only when you want your puppy to become excited and playful. Your puppy can sense your feelings through the tone of voice you use, and will reflect those feelings in its actions. When you feel relaxed and confident, so will your puppy.

If you are upset with your puppy, don't yell and scream—just drop your voice to a deep, stern tone. The most threatening sound uttered by a dog is a very deep, low growl that is often barely audible. Couple this with a stern, direct look and a body posture that is very tall, straight and stiff, and your puppy will know without a doubt that you mean business.

When you give a command, do so with a confident voice of average volume. If your tone and demeanor convey that you expect your puppy to do what you tell it to do, it will gladly cooperate. If you lack confidence and sound or look like you don't expect your puppy to do what it is told, it will gladly cooperate with that, too. It is not so much *what* you say, but *how* you say it—with both your voice and your body.

Your puppy will respond because that is what it instinctively looks for in other dogs. You can "program in" commands, but to truly relate to your puppy, talk to it in a manner that it instinctively understands using body language and appropriate voice tones.

When you leave your puppy at the groomer, kennel, or even at home when you go to work and attempt to reassure it with a whiney, "It's OK, I'll be back," or "You'll be all right, don't be afraid," you are actually telling your puppy that everything is *not* all right and that it should be upset and afraid.

Your puppy is going to respond to the stress you are feeling at leaving it behind, not the words you say. Your puppy may whine back at you, which may puff up your ego with the feeling that it can't live without you, but this is actually your issue and has nothing to do with your puppy. It will have a fascinating day, be quite content and happy until your return, and will not suffer any of the fears or anxieties that you are telling it to have. Just say, "See you later," in a calm, but chipper, voice and walk away. Your puppy may bark a bit while you are still in sight, but will soon quit, settle in, and enjoy all the new sights and smells or just go to sleep.

This applies to vet visits, too. Have you ever sat in the vet's office and watched an owner trying to calm a distraught dog that is whining and obviously distressed? The owner most likely conditioned this behavior. The dog senses its owner's worry and anxiety and then becomes stressed itself in response. Had the owner maintained a calm, positive demeanor, the dog would respond in kind and vet visits would be a pleasurable experience. Take heart: Most dogs have a much higher pain threshold than humans—a little pinch from a needle is barely felt and is over in a second.

Teaching Your Puppy Words

Your puppy's name is simply a sound it learns to associate with giving its attention to you, so use it whenever you want its attention. Every word is a unique sound that your puppy eventually learns from your use of consistent and repeated associations. For this reason, you want to imbue meaning into every word you say to your puppy.

Many words or commands can be taught very simply by saying a word—the same word each time—when your puppy is in the act of doing something. For example, whenever your puppy is almost completely into a sitting position, say "sit." As soon as it is fully in the sit position, lavish praise. Or, when your puppy is almost into the down position, say "down" and again praise when it is completely in the position.

After regularly hearing the sound of a word connected with a particular action, followed by your praise, you puppy will become conditioned to respond to the word. The number of words a dog can learn by using word association in this manner is limitless. You can give a name to each of your puppy's toys when it picks one up.

Say "walk" while grabbing your puppy's leash and then taking it outside.

Ask "Who's home!?" at the moment your significant other opens the garage door after being away. Once learned, your puppy will know exactly what or who to expect when you say the trigger phrase. The list goes on and on.

Always choose a word or phrase that states what you want and then visualize what you want to see from your puppy. Example: You are out walking your puppy and it is pulling. Instead of saying, "Don't pull" which has your focus and emphasis on "pulling" and will make your puppy pull more, say, "Stop pulling" or "Easy." This puts your focus and emphasis on "stop" and will make your puppy slow down and walk with a looser lead.

Another example: use "off" instead of "don't jump." State your desire in the positive and avoid the negative. The idea of stating commands in the positive is a mirror to the idea of training with "positive reinforcement." State a command in a manner that clearly states what you want your puppy to do, rather than using the multitude of statements of what not to do with the repetitive and meaningless use of the word "don't," as in "don't" do this and "don't" do that.

You can "foolproof" a command by giving it in many tones of voice, from various positions, and have your puppy comply. Your puppy then becomes programmed to understand the command without connecting it to your body language. A dog that has learned through this type of repetitious training will comply with commands given in the softest of whispers. Teaching your puppy in this manner is done in gradual stages over time, with consistent enforcement of the command under a variety of circumstances.

While your puppy is young and learning, the word "no" should be reserved for use as a forceful sound in an emergency to distract your puppy from possible injury or danger. You want the sound to immediately grab your puppy's attention with alarm and authority. Exuberant praise must immediately follow when the puppy stops whatever it was doing. It will quickly learn what "no" means when used under such conditions, as somewhat of a by-product to positive reinforcement, which you will then be able to use more often when your puppy is older.

During early training, it is ill-advised to use "no" to correct or stop every infraction. Using the same word repeatedly without associating any specific meaning to it makes it ineffective and pointless. If all you say to your puppy is "no," "no," "no," and it hasn't a clue exactly what "no" means, you are failing to teach it anything. Besides, in using positive reinforcement for regular training, "no" is not part of the program.

Your puppy is much more easily taught what TO DO, rather than what NOT TO DO. Think about it: For the dozens of things you don't want your puppy to do, there is usually only one thing per situation that you do want it to do. Consider all the things your puppy would like to chew on: cushions, the newspaper, your sock, or house plants. Instead of saying "Don't eat the plant," "Don't chew the newspaper," and so on, you can use one command in all situations indicating to your puppy what you want: "Leave it" alone. In any of these situations, you can separate your puppy from the item saying "Leave it," followed by offering it one of its chew toys, and praising as soon as your puppy grabs the toy.

Praise positive behaviors to encourage your puppy to repeat them. Through repetition, with the use of a consistent command word with the same positive action over and over, your puppy learns the meaning behind the words—much the same way a child learns. After your puppy has truly grasped the meaning of a word, you will be able to use it in a wider array of situations as your puppy matures.

Your puppy will learn additional words, as well as routines and body language on its own. It is constantly observing your every movement, listening to your conversations, and will pick out those actions or words that repeatedly relate to a particular outcome. Eventually, your puppy will amaze you when it anticipates your next step from having watched your routines.

Playful Biting

One of the first facts you must accept is that your puppy is going to use its mouth. Like a child using his or her hands, a puppy uses its mouth constantly to learn about its world and the things in it. The constant chewing, mouthing, and biting is a trait that your puppy will outgrow with age and learning. Also, keep in mind that your puppy has new teeth growing, which is painful, so it wants to gnaw, chew, and apply pressure to its gums to alleviate the pain. Your goal is to teach your puppy how to use its mouth in an acceptable manner.

Many people make the mistake of tapping a puppy on the muzzle to make it stop gnawing and biting. The fact is that this will only encourage more biting. Although the initial surprise of a tap may at first stop your puppy, don't be deceived. As you continue to bop its nose each time it mouths your hand, your puppy will interpret this as encouragement to play even rougher.

From its point of view, your hand just became a toy. As discussed earlier, also refrain from saying "no," because your puppy will be unable to connect the word to its actions. Biting and mouthing at this young age is a strongly instinctive trait, one that cannot be eliminated but can be controlled and will eventually be outgrown and come to a natural stop.

The best method of discouraging your puppy from constantly mouthing your hand is to offer it a toy. Immediately praise your puppy when it grabs the toy instead of your hand. Keep plenty of toys available, and rotate them to keep your puppy interested. Just like a child, a puppy gets bored with the same old thing.

It is normal for your puppy to want to wrestle and rough-house, nipping and holding your hand in its mouth. If you do not want to play with your puppy in this manner, you will need to direct its urge to grab and mouth to a different target, such as a toy. If your puppy consistently ignores the toy after several attempts, you must stop the play and walk away. Yes, it will be difficult to walk away from your puppy when you want to play as much as it does, but your puppy will soon learn that the only way you will continue play is by including the toy.

Wrestling during playtime is perfectly acceptable so long as you are setting and maintaining the tone of your puppy's enthusiasm. You are your puppy's play partner if there are no other animals in the household. Gentle wrestling between dogs is natural. By wrestling and acting like a dog, your puppy will bond to you even more closely.

There is a definite competitive nature to tug-of-war games. Just like a child, a puppy figures anything you have must be better than what it has. Certainly, this is how tug-of-war started—coveting thy neighbor's belongings!

You must be careful in playing this game with your puppy. Keep it gentle. Avoid yanking a toy from a puppy, as you could hurt its teeth. Also avoid being overly rough about winning the toy from your puppy, because this will make it become rougher in its play. This game is a good opportunity to teach "out" or "let go." After a bit of actual tugging, tell you puppy to let go and take the toy from it. You are teaching the puppy that you are in charge and get to have the toy whenever you want. However, an occasional win for your puppy will certainly keep the game more fun—everyone needs to win at least once in a while, or else what's the point?

If your puppy is tenacious in its mouthing and biting, behave as an older dog would by gently but firmly squeezing its muzzle to make it let go. If that's not enough, you can take a firm hold of the puppy around its ribcage, lifting its front legs or whole body off the ground, which puts it under your complete power and authority. Once your puppy relaxes and you return it to the ground, and it still continues its rough play-biting, walk away and return to play after it calms down.

Keep repeating this until it learns that only gentle play or no biting will result in continued playtime. If you notice that excessive biting occurs at the same time, under the same conditions, or in the same place, then change that situation! For example, perhaps your puppy's biting becomes extreme after the evening meal while playing in the kitchen. Rather than continuing this routine, take your puppy for a walk after eating. Alter the situation and you're likely to eliminate the undesirable behavior.

Housebreaking and Crate Training

To a dog raised utilizing its inherent instincts, training is merely an extension of natural behaviors to accommodate for life within a human household. Because canines are naturally cave dwellers, they are normally very clean animals. They prefer not to soil their living area.

If your puppy was raised by a reputable breeder, it was kept in a clean environment large enough for part of the area to be set up for eating and sleeping and part

covered with papers or other absorbent material. Such a setup allows for natural instincts to kick in and the puppy will housebreak itself by choosing to eliminate on the papers instead of in its sleeping area. The breeder will transfer a puppy to a larger and larger area as it grows and, if possible, give it outdoor access. By the time your puppy arrives at its new home, with a little care—and following these suggestions—housebreaking will be a snap.

Because of its cave-dwelling instincts, a dog looks at a crate as a haven, not as the human concept of a cage or prison. In fact, the most important thing you can do for the mental and emotional security of your puppy is crate training. The crate becomes its private space, a security blanket and a place where it can go to rest, relax, and be left alone. This is very important to a dog, especially one living in a household with children or much activity.

NEVER put your puppy in its crate to punish it. The crate must stay a happy place. Your puppy may appear to resent the crate at first, but it's separation from you that upsets it. To aid in quickly acclimating your puppy to the crate, keep its water inside and feed it in the crate for the first several weeks. Place the crate in a location that is quiet yet still allows your puppy to see and be near you.

The housebreaking process begins when your puppy first arrives home. Hopefully it has been raised in clean conditions and has never had to override its instincts to stay that way. Wake up earlier so that you have plenty of time to feed your puppy and take it outside to relieve itself thoroughly before you leave the house for the day.

A puppy between the ages of 8 and 10 weeks is physically incapable of reliable bladder control, and it is important to maintain patience and take it outside every 30 minutes while it is awake and active. If you must be gone for long periods of time, you may need to arrange an area large enough to place papers for the puppy to relieve itself, along with a clean sleeping area.

At 10 to 12 weeks of age, a puppy should have more control as its body and muscles continue to develop and strengthen. It will be better able to control its bladder all day while you are away.

Unlike we who live by our watches, dogs have no concept of time. You see this when, whether you leave for five minutes or five hours, the homecoming greeting you get is the same. If your puppy soils the crate the first time or two that you are away, just clean up and forget it. Generally, in a few days, it will realize the necessity of controlling itself and acclimate to your schedule.

Once your puppy is old enough and has the physical maturity to hold its bladder, the crate should supply just enough room for your puppy to stand and turn around comfortably. If the crate offers too much room, your puppy may just relieve itself at one end and sleep in the other.

Relinquish any ideas about punishing your puppy during the housebreaking process. Urination and defecation are normal and necessary. To offer punishment in response for performing a bodily need is absurd. Your objective is to teach your puppy to perform this function in an area of your choosing, i.e., outside.

Refrain from lengthy admonishment if your puppy is in the midst of urinating inside the house. Your first reaction when you see your puppy eliminating in the house is naturally going to be to voice a loud expletive or "no!" to be immediately followed by literally picking up your puppy as it's going (which should stop at this point), whisk it outside, and set it down to finish. When finished, offer praise and return inside. Quickly clean the mishap and finish by using an enzymatic odor-eliminating product available at any pet store or through any pet supply catalog.

During the first several weeks, be sure to take your puppy outside often. Always take it out first thing in the morning, after any period of sleep, after eating and play sessions, before bedtime, and any time it appears to be restless or is obviously looking for a spot to relieve itself, which is indicated by persistent sniffing and circling.

When you arrive home or first get up in the morning, do NOT rile your puppy by talking to it in a high-pitched, excited voice. Remain silent or speak in a normal tone and take it outside immediately. Offer praise when it "goes."

If you wish for your puppy to relieve itself in a specific location in the yard, always take it there. You will achieve greater success if you pick a spot in your yard farthest from your house, which is in line with your puppy's natural instincts. Teach it to go on command by saying your specific command word, such as "Hurry up" or "Go potty" each time your puppy is in position to eliminate. For the future, this will speed things up and is quite handy when you go on trips, or as a way to let your dog know that it is OK for it to relieve itself in a new area.

Submissive urination is normal in a young puppy. Should your puppy urinate when it is being greeted, you need to understand that this is an involuntary and normal response to the dominant members of the pack. Never discipline your puppy when this occurs because doing so only makes the problem worse. Follow the directions above, and as your puppy gains confidence in itself and develops trust in you, it will outgrow the behavior.

Until your puppy is housebroken, you must keep it in sight at all times while loose in the house. When left free to wander, it could pick an out-of-the way spot to relieve itself or begin chewing on unacceptable items, such as furniture or clothing. If you are unable to watch your puppy for even one minute, place it in its crate until you have the time to devote to it without distraction.

Pay attention to the signs that tell you it is looking for a place to relieve itself, as described earlier. Also, remember that dogs are creatures of habit and routine, so the sooner you develop a regular routine for feeding, eating, and sleeping, the easier it will be for your puppy to adjust to its new home.

Another major problem you avoid by crating your puppy when it is to be left alone is the development of destructive behavior. Behaviors such as tearing up doors, chewing furniture, and shredding carpeting are all associated with boredom and/or anxiety. Keep your puppy crated while you are away to prevent mischief, and you and your puppy will be able to enjoy a pleasant homecoming and share time together happily.

Leaving your young, uneducated puppy loose and unsupervised is dangerous to its health, as well. Consider the potential risks, such as live electrical cords that are at perfect chewing height, poisonous plants, and knick-knacks to be ingested or choked on.

For you and your puppy's well-being, give it a safe place and crate-train it. Once your puppy has learned proper social etiquette, you can decide when and how much freedom to allow as it continues to mature.

Feeding Time

Teaching your puppy manners regarding food is an absolute must. This brief section offers a few tips on promoting good manners and preventing problems surrounding feeding time.

Any dog can be both possessive and protective. This pertains not only to family and home, but also to food, toys, and bones. It is imperative to teach your puppy from the start that any display of possessiveness toward a family member for taking these items from it is totally unacceptable. This lesson must be reinforced throughout your dog's life. When children are present in the household, this rule becomes even more important.

The easiest way to teach your puppy good manners is to make a practice of adding bits of food to its bowl while it is eating. Every member of the household should take turns doing this. It allows you to put your hand near your puppy's mouth while it's eating. Through the reward of more food, your puppy learns that it is beneficial to have you near its food.

Some training methods recommend taking away the food bowl and then replacing it after a few seconds, but this only causes the puppy to become stressed about losing its food—a negative reaction that should be avoided. When your puppy becomes comfortable with you near its food, there will be no problem with removing the bowl in the future.

The same theory applies to toys. Never play hide-and-seek with a very young puppy, as it will not understand that the toy is merely out of sight and will become stressed that it is gone forever. To promote active and pleasant play, have several toys at your fingertips. Hand your puppy the first toy and let it chew for a minute, then offer another toy. As the first toy is dropped, give a command, such as "out." Offer praise for giving up the first toy. Your puppy is at ease because it got a new toy for releasing the first toy and you have just created a pleasant experience that can be expanded as your puppy gets older. Soon it will be giving up its toy to you to get praise and initiate play.

Your puppy's attention span will lengthen, and you will be able to start tossing the toy, which it will gleefully retrieve. Also, by handing toys to your puppy, it learns what items are acceptable and that only items offered by the pack leader are okay to chew on. Your puppy will learn that objects not offered by you are not its to chew.

A common mistake many people make is giving a puppy an old shoe or sock as a toy. Your puppy will not know the difference between old or new socks and shoes, and you will be heartbroken when your puppy ruins your best pair of dress shoes after it has been allowed to demolish your old tennies.

You can, however, make an old sock different from a new sock by tying a knot in it. This difference will be enough for your puppy to learn which socks it may have and which are to be left alone. It is not feasible to make an understandable difference between old and new shoes, so it is best never to give your puppy shoes to chew on.

If you frequently have visitors or people who will be caring for your puppy in your absence, it is a good idea to involve them with your puppy's food and toys. This practice will give you comfort if you ever have to hire a dog sitter.

Coming When Called

It is possible to begin teaching your puppy to come when called, even at a very young age. The process is begun when the breeder first begins to supplement the litter's feedings. Just before putting down the food dish, the breeder calls in a happy voice, "Pup, pup, pup," and when the puppies come, they get food. When you get your puppy home, just add its name into your call, and be sure to reward it with food, or lots of love and praise, and in the future it will come to you willingly.

Never call your puppy to discipline it for something it has done wrong. This is a very common mistake. If someone you trusted were to call you over and then punish you, how long before you stopped coming to the call?

Always call your puppy in a happy voice, praising it immediately when it even looks in your direction, then call again and praise when it comes to you. Coming to you should always be a positive experience for your puppy. Don't command your puppy to come to you in a harsh or forceful voice. Rather, lift your voice to a happy tone. Practice with the whole family by sitting in a circle and calling your puppy to each family member one at a time, rewarding it lavishly for responding.

Another good exercise is "follow me." Walk and have your puppy follow at your side by talking happily to it, patting your leg, and praising when it is at your side. It is an excellent preliminary exercise in teaching how to "Heel." If you practice this often and in different areas with distractions, you can get voice control over your puppy at a very young age and maintain this into adulthood.

It is worth stating that your puppy should always be on a lead when not in an enclosed area. To prevent possible injury—and by law in many states—the puppy should be under control at all times. Retractable leashes are best used after you puppy has learned how to walk properly on-lead, without pulling.

Jumping Up

One of the most common complaints from dog owners is that their puppy jumps up. Understand what this behavior means to the dog, and then you will know how to avoid it. There are many reasons for a puppy to jump up in greeting. One of the ways that a puppy establishes its dominance among its littermates is to tower over another by standing and placing its front paws on the other's back. If the other puppy accepts and submits to this posturing, the puppy that is posturing becomes the dominant one.

If you are sitting on the floor and you allow your puppy to stand with its front feet on your back or shoulders, you are sending the message to your puppy that it ranks higher than you. This illustrates just one of the many ways that the misunderstanding of canine body language can inadvertently cause problems in the future relationship between dog and owner.

Conversely, a puppy also jumps up because, in the canine world, it is a natural behavior for a puppy to greet adult dogs by licking their muzzles. By doing this, a puppy is displaying its submissiveness to the pack leader and requesting food. After returning from the hunt or eating its bowl of food, canines in the wild or mother dogs in a breeder's home will regurgitate food for their puppies as an automatic response to the persistent licking of their muzzles.

The easiest way to avoid the problem of jumping up is to teach your puppy from day one always to sit or stand before being petted. This is very easy to teach. As you and your puppy come into contact, maintain an upright position, talking to your puppy in a calm, normal voice. If your puppy jumps up, gently push it into a sitting or standing position while voicing a command word, such as "off." While it is in the desired position of sitting or standing, pet and praise. Repeat this scenario consistently and your puppy will soon learn that only by controlling its excitement will it be rewarded with attention.

Have friends and even strangers practice this with your puppy. When involving others in your puppy's training, you must advise them of their role ahead of time. Teaching your puppy and your friends at the same time will result in poor results and confusion for your puppy.

Not jumping up and other positive behaviors, like waiting to go through a door until the "okay" command is given, are all examples of developing clear communication and understanding. If everyone in the household reinforces good behaviors unanimously and consistently, you will be thrilled with the results and the ease with which they are accomplished.

The old notion that you wait to attend an obedience class when your puppy turns six months old—and has already become a difficult and intolerable dog—is false. If you live with your dog properly from day one, obedience training will not be necessary, but instead can be just another fun thing you and your four-legged friend can do together later on and that serves as an excellent socialization tool.

The average canine has the IQ of a 3- to 5-year-old child, which makes it quite capable of intelligent interaction with its human family. Just like a child, it only has to be taught to use its brain, expected to do so, and be rewarded for doing it. Good behavior is a way of life, not a response to commands.

Begging at the Table and Other Pesky Habits

Common sense dictates that you never feed your puppy from the table if you do not want it staring at you during your meal or salivating on visitors. If you do so even occasionally, be prepared for it to embarrass you by being an absolute pest during get-togethers.

The good behavior of a beautiful dog can be a credit to you in any social situation. If you wish to give your puppy table scraps, place them in its food bowl after you are completely finished eating your meal. If your puppy understands "go lay down" as a phrase used before bedtime, the same phrase may work just as well in this situation, where you want your puppy away from the dinner table and lying down quietly.

To keep your puppy off the furniture and continuing this good behavior into doggy adulthood, only hold it on your lap when you are sitting on the floor. You must realize that your puppy doesn't understand the concept of "just this one time." In its mind, a behavior that is allowed once is simply allowed—anytime, anywhere.

To avoid having your 100-pound adult dog bounding through the house, barking, and grabbing things to chew and play with, don't play such games with it in the house when it's a cute, little, 10-pound puppy. You must decide how much play to allow inside the house. Anything you will not want your adult dog to do later cannot be allowed from your puppy. It is your responsibility to decide ahead of time what behaviors will be acceptable to you and then teach your puppy accordingly.

Most of this is only common sense. Unfortunately, many pet owners don't figure it out. Undesired behaviors are why so many dogs end up being kept out in the backyard, placed in new homes, given up to a shelter, or, even worse, put down, because their owners couldn't deal with their adult dog's bad, puppy-like behaviors.

Raise your puppy with sensibility and patience, and become the envy of every dog owner you know. Better yet, when these methods have been proven, share your knowledge with other pet owners so that everyone can enjoy the delight of sharing their lives with a canine companion.

Outdoor Time

Accompany your puppy whenever it is outside. If your puppy barks, whether at passers-by, squirrels, or falling leaves, always check out why it is vocalizing. When you identify the source, give about a three-bark limit, and then stop your puppy by simply distracting it or by breaking its line of vision to the object it is barking at, and offer praise the moment your puppy stops barking.

Random barking is like the boy who cried wolf: you will soon ignore it, and some day, it will be important that you do not. Random barking also is a nuisance to your neighbors. Make your dog a good citizen, and if at some point, it uncharacteristically persists in barking, your neighbors may be alert enough to save your life or your house by listening to its call for help.

When your puppy is older and you plan to have it spending any length of time outside unsupervised, it is best to have either a kennel area or a fence that it cannot jump or climb over. Dogs that are tied out or tethered leave them vulnerable to the possibility of the tether becoming tangled around the dog or an object in its area, and leaving it unable to avoid or escape a dangerous

situation. Tethers can also snap and break, allowing your dog to wander.

In-ground, electric fences have their uses, but there are disadvantages. For one, the device may keep your dog in, but it isn't going to keep invaders out. A small dog unattended outside is easy prey for a passing predator. Another point to consider is that a strong dog will bear the pain of passing the electric barrier if it is determined to reach something beyond the fence, and won't likely be so determined when it wants to return to your yard. Now your dog is roaming loose in the neighborhood. Solid fencing is the best method to keep your dog safe when it is outside.

If you are thinking of having your puppy become a full-time "outdoor dog," please reconsider! Dogs are pack animals. You are their pack. If you shut them away from your home and family, they will be miserable and generally resort to barking, digging, or other destructive habits. Also, a dog in the backyard cannot warn you of a thief coming through the front window. Nor can it learn the etiquette needed to become an enjoyable companion. If you have no intention of spending time with or educating your dog, buy a goldfish instead. Dogs deserve and require more than sitting as an ornament in a backyard.

The Tail End

Acquiring a puppy is easy. Puppies are cute and cuddly and their silly antics are adorable. And then, very quickly, they grow up, are less cute, become more independent and those silly antics have become annoying.

When a puppy reaches that trying adolescent age of one to two years of age is when up to 40 percent of owners (based on available statistics) relinquish their puppy to a shelter, send back to the breeder, or have it euthanized. This happens due to an owner's lack of commitment, lack of canine understanding, and purchasing a puppy on a whim, rather than making an informed and educated decision about obtaining the type of puppy that best suites the person's ability and lifestyle.

Making the decision to own a dog requires sincere contemplation and an honest assessment of the commitment that will be required for the years, possibly decades, to come. Investing time and effort during the first couple years of your puppy's life will help create a thoroughly enjoyable relationship between you and your puppy—

ideally, a relationship built on respect, appreciation, and very importantly, a solid foundation of clear communication and understanding.

Every relationship has its ups and downs, hurdles, and challenges. Hopefully, the information and examples contained in this book have supplied you with new ideas and perspectives that will assist you in developing a lasting relationship with your canine companion—from choosing the correct breed and the correct breeder of your puppy, to supplying basic physical needs, and the optimal environment for learning. Your puppy can only become your ideal companion if given the guidance and nurturing needed to learn the many and varied lessons that are required and necessary.

Having a dog, or any animal in your life to care for, love, and be loved by, is a privilege. It is your responsibility to make your puppy an ideal puppy and then experience the joy that comes from creating a successful relationship with your furry friend.

May the tips in this book serve you well.

Additional Resources

www.akc.org—AKC.org offers information on dog breeds, competition events, club search for training and services, dog ownership and registration.

www.cesarsway.com—Dog training DVDs, books, articles and video tutorials by dog behavior specialist, Cesar Millan.

www.clickertraining.com—Popularized by author Karen Pryor, clicker training is a fabulous and effective way to improve the relationship and understanding between you and your pet.

www.naiaonline.org—National Animal Interest Alliance The mission of NAIA is to promote animal welfare to strengthen the human-animal bond, and safeguard the rights of responsible animal owners, enthusiasts, and professionals through research, public information and sound public policy.

www.naturalrearing.com—This site exists to provide information on Natural Rearing and alternative, holistic, complementary healthcare for pets.

www.offa.org—OFA is a non-profit organization that collates and disseminates
information concerning orthopedic and genetic disease of animals.

www.pennhip.org—PennHIP (an acronym for "University of Pennsylvania Hip
Improvement Program") is a diagnostic technique for evaluating the hips of dogs for laxity.

www.superpuppy.com —Books, videos, tips, on puppy training and dog training. Canine behavior help for pet owners, dog trainers and veterinarians.

www.ukcdogs.com—The United Kennel Club, established in 1898, is the largest all-breed performance dog registry in the world, registering dogs from all 50 states and 25 other countries. It offers people a multitude of events to do with their dogs.

www.vmdb.org – CERF is a centralized, national registry of dogs certified free
of heritable eye disease by members of the American College of Veterinary Ophthalmologists

About the Author

R esiding in a peaceful, rural area of Illinois, Danielle Gutelius lives a quiet and simple life. She spends her available hours as a hobby breeder, raising Akitas of exceptional quality for the conformation show ring, as well as companion dogs with loyal and affectionate temperaments. During the last twenty years, she has taken great joy in rearing and exhibiting her dogs with much success. Her passions, in addition to her dogs, include all things relating to nature and the environment, as well as animal communication, EFT, and other forms of energy work to assist animals and their people. Please visit her website at www.tanagerakitas.com.